Order this book online at www.trafford.com
or email orders@trafford.com

Most Trafford titles are also available at major online book retailers.

Printed in the United States of America.

ISBN: 978-1-4907-4668-5 (sc)
        978-1-4907-4669-2 (e)

Library of Congress Control Number: 2014916458

Our mission is to efficiently provide the world's finest, most comprehensive book publishing service, enabling every author to experience success. To find out how to publish your book, your way, and have it available worldwide, visit us online at www.trafford.com

Any people depicted in stock imagery provided by Thinkstock are models, and such images are being used for illustrative purposes only.
Certain stock imagery © Thinkstock.

Trafford rev. 09/18/2014

www.trafford.com
North America & international
toll-free: 1 888 232 4444 (USA & Canada)
fax: 812 355 4082

I

AM

WORTH

THE

WAIT

By: Lindsay M. Warren, MD

Rachel,
You are Worth
the Wait!

2025

This book is dedicated to our daughter, **Grace Kaydence Warren**. Daddy and I love you very much!! You are our special treasure!!

I would like to give special thanks to **Whitney Tarver** (my sister), **Elice Browne** (my friend) and **Gareth Warren** (my husband). Your collective assistance with this children's book has been so helpful. I appreciate your insight and attention to detail.

I would like to thank God for His inspiration. I will never forget those special words spoken softly to me: "Lindsay, you are worth the wait."

Mommy and Daddy always share encouraging words with me. They build my self-esteem and help me to understand my worth and value.

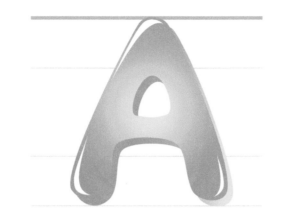

Mommy says, I am **A**wesome...

Daddy says, I am **B**rilliant...

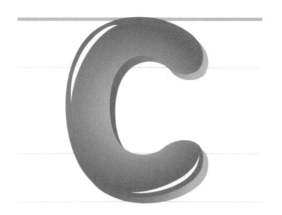

Mommy says, I am Creative...

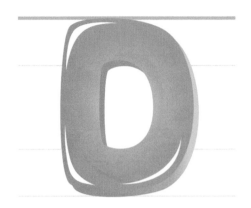

Daddy says, I am Delightful...

Mommy says, I am Excellent...

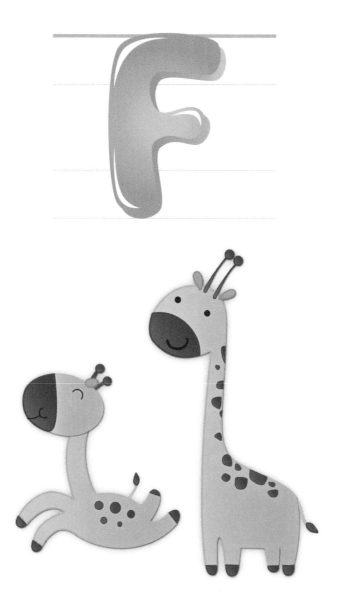

Daddy says, I am **F**earless...

Mommy says, I am **G**ifted...

Daddy says, I am **H**elpful...

Mommy says, I am **I**ntelligent...

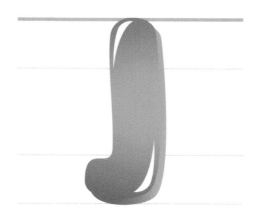

Daddy says, I am Joyful...

K

Mommy says, I am **K**ind...

Daddy says, I am Loved...

Mommy says, I am **M**arvelous...

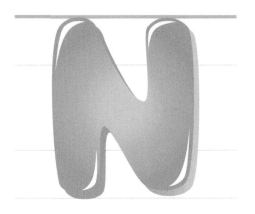

Daddy says, I am **N**ice...

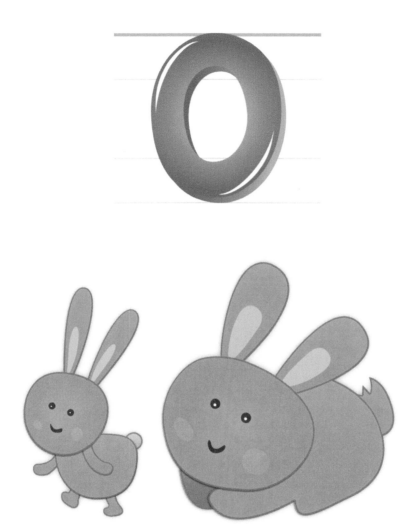

Mommy says, I am

Outstanding...

Daddy says, I am **P**recious...

Mommy says, I am
Quite clever...

Daddy says, I am **R**are...

Mommy says, I am Special...

T

Daddy says, I am Talented...

Mommy says, I am **U**nique...

Daddy says, I am **V**ery polite...

Mommy says, I am **W**onderful...

Daddy says, I am e**X**quisite...

Y

Mommy says, I am

extraordinar Y ...

Z

Daddy says, I am amaZing...

And, God says, **I am a great TREASURE** that is loved by Him and . . .

I AM WORTH THE WAIT!!!

CPSIA information can be obtained at www.ICGtesting.com
Printed in the USA
LVOW02s2314011014

406795LV00003B/6/P

9 781490 746685